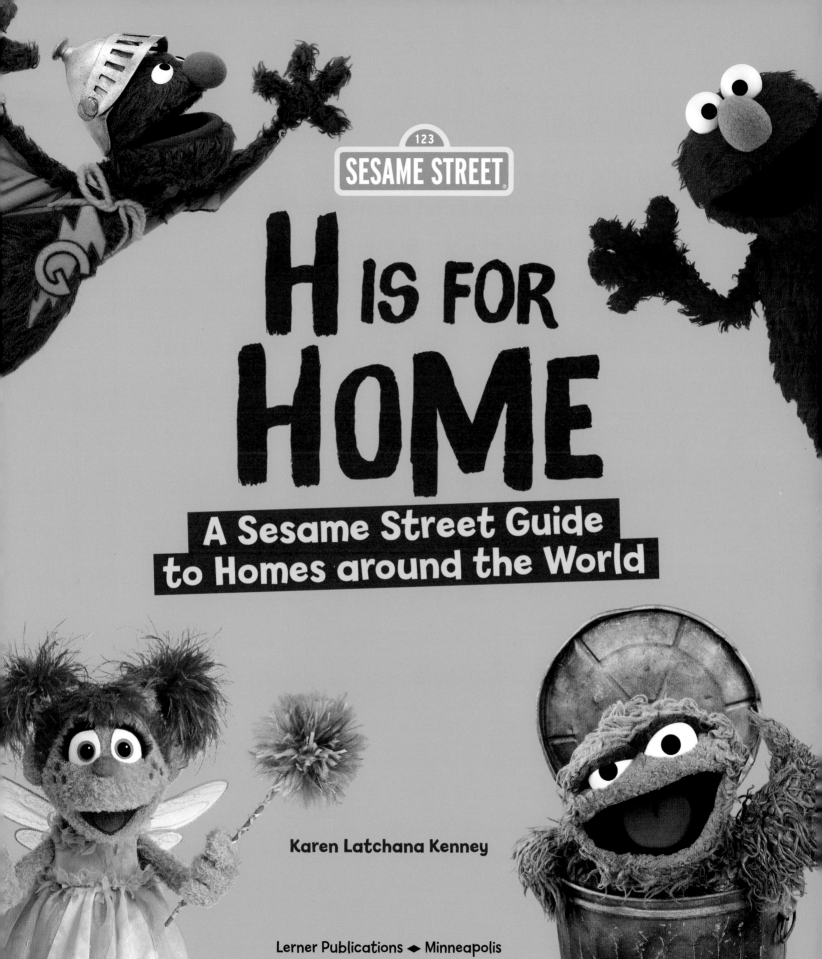

SESAME STREET
123

H IS FOR HOME

A Sesame Street Guide to Homes around the World

Karen Latchana Kenney

Lerner Publications ◆ Minneapolis

Big Bird lives in a nest. Oscar lives in a trash can. Bert and Ernie live in an apartment at 123 Sesame Street. All around the world, people live in different kinds of homes. But wherever you call home, your friends on Sesame Street want you to remember the most important thing: Home is where the love lives.

Sincerely,

The Editors at Sesame Workshop

Table of Contents

Homes Everywhere

Homes come in all shapes and sizes.

This apartment building is filled with many homes.

Lots of neighbors live here.

A family lives in this house.

Families eat, work, and play together.

A duplex is two homes in one building.

Neighbors live right next to each other.
They share a porch.

Stilts keep these homes high above the ground. They protect the homes from wet ground during the rainy season.

Families can store things below the house when it's dry.

See those thick clay walls? This is an adobe home.

The clay walls keep cool air inside this adobe home.

This home stays cool in the hot, dry desert.

Grass grows on the roof and walls of these houses.

It keeps warm air inside the homes.

A round home is made of mud and wood.
It has one big room.

Some round homes have a roof made of dry grass.

This home can be taken down and moved when the family decides to move.

A yurt is a home you can fold up. It's a tent with a wood frame.

Its walls are made of fabric.

Some homes can set sail!
A houseboat floats in the water.

But most of the time, it stays at a dock.

Where are these homes? They're deep underground!

Living underground keeps families cool in the desert heat.

People make homes in many places.
But a home is not just a place.

A World of Homes

Use this map to explore different homes around the world!

NORTH AMERICA

New Mexico, US

Guyana

SOUTH AMERICA

Brazil

England, UK

Mongolia

Iceland

ASIA

EUROPE

AFRICA

Ivory
Coast

Spain

South
Africa

AUSTRALIA

ANTARCTICA

Picture Glossary

adobe: a building material made of clay that is dried in the sun

dock: a place where a boat or ship regularly parks

stilts: posts that support a home so it stays high above the ground or water

yurt: a round tent home that is made from wood and animal skins or fabric

Family Homelessness

Not everyone has a place to live. Some people lose their homes. A shelter gives families a safe place to stay for a short time. A refugee camp may help them move to a safer place. Their homes are wherever their families are. Home is where the love lives.

Find out more about homelessness here: https://sesamestreetincommunities.org/topics /family-homelessness/.

Index

Lerner Publications Company
An imprint of Lerner Publishing Group, Inc.
241 First Avenue North
Minneapolis, MN 55401 USA

For reading levels and more information, look up this title at www.lernerbooks.com.

Main body text set in Billy Infant. Typeface provided by SparkyType.

Editor: Allison Juda **Designer:** Emily Harris **Lerner team:** Martha Kranes

Library of Congress Cataloging-in-Publication Data

Names: Kenney, Karen Latchana, author.
Title: H is for home : a Sesame Street ® guide to homes around the world / Karen Latchana Kenney.
Description: Minneapolis : Lerner Publications, [2021] | Includes index. | Audience: Ages: 4-8 | Audience: Grades: K-1 | Summary: "From apartments and houses to houseboats and yurts—home is where you feel loved and safe. The characters of Sesame Street take readers around the world to learn more about how kids live across the globe."— Provided by publisher.
Identifiers: LCCN 2019045828 (print) | LCCN 2019045829 (ebook) | ISBN 9781541590014 (library binding) | ISBN 9781728413761 (paperback) | ISBN 9781728400655 (ebook)
Subjects: LCSH: Sesame Street (Television program)—Juvenile literature. | Dwellings—Juvenile literature. | Housing—Juvenile literature. | Architecture, Domestic—Juvenile literature.
Classification: LCC GT172 .K33 2021 (print) | LCC GT172 (ebook) | DDC 392.3/6—dc23

LC record available at https://lccn.loc.gov/2019045828
LC ebook record available at https://lccn.loc.gov/2019045829

Manufactured in the United States of America
1-47517-48055-3/5/2020

Photo Acknowledgments

Image credits: Gerard van den Akker/Getty Images, p. 4 (top left); Ramesh Thadani/Getty Images, p. 4 (top right); Laura Olivas/Getty Images, p. 4 (bottom); miguelangelortega/Getty Images, pp. 6, 29; NicolasMcComber/Getty Images, p. 7; Thelma Gatuzzo/Getty Images, pp. 8, 28; PeopleImages/Getty Images, p. 9; Leisa Tyler/LightRocket/Getty Images, p. 10; Marje/Getty Images, p. 11; espiegle/iStock/Getty Images, pp. 12, 28, 30; Created by MaryAnne Nelson/Getty Images, p. 13; ivanastar/Getty Images, pp. 14, 28, 30; JannHuizenga/Getty Images, p. 15; RbbrDckyBK/iStock/Getty Images, pp. 16, 17, 29; Gerard van den Akker/Getty Images, pp. 18, 29; Bartosz Hadyniak/Getty Images, p. 19; Claudio Rampinini/Shutterstock.com, pp. 20, 29, 30; Jen Seiser/Getty Images, p. 21; Apexphotos/Getty Images, pp. 22, 23, 29, 30; tjs11/iStock/Getty Images, pp. 24, 25, 29; MoMo Productions/Getty Images, p. 26.

Cover images: molloykeith/Getty Images; RobertCrum/Getty Images; Gosiek-B/Getty Images; deberarr/Getty Images.